# ACCIDENTALLY VEGAN

# ITALIAN SALADS

Many people contributed to this work including Sara Virgilio, Hanna Elhori, Rita Arra, Rachele Puntel, Erica Riva, Shannon Parker, Nancy Soper, Mia Caruso, Michael Caruso, and Sofia Caruso.

ISBN-10 : 1736956604

ISBN-13 : 978-1736956601

Created, designed, and published in the USA.

# ACCIDENTALLY VEGAN

# ITALIAN SALADS

*Modern versions of 32 scrumptious Italian salads that always were and always will be vegan*

Giovanni Caruso

*For all the vegans and wannabe vegans out there.*

*Buon appetito!*

# CONTENTS

# INTRODUCTION

Welcome to the second book in the *Accidentally Vegan* series! In the first book, 30 vegan Italian soups were presented, and we now turn our attention to vegan Italian salads. The salads in this book were collected because they are vegan and because they are Italian but also because they do not require substitutions or omissions to earn their vegan designation. That is, they are *accidentally* vegan. No doubt there are many vegan salads, Italian and otherwise, that include meat, dairy, and egg substitutes in place of the original non-vegan ingredients. These ingredients and these salads have their place, but to be included in this book the salads had to be vegan by nature rather than by alteration. Researching, testing, selecting, and presenting such recipes is my mission for the *Accidentally Vegan* series. Before we get to the recipes, I've written a few words on salad dressings, beans, other ingredients, and the best way to use this book.

# SALAD DRESSINGS

All of the salads in this book are dressed with what the Italians call *condimenti* (salad dressings). Sometimes it is as simple as a drizzle of olive oil, but usually it consists of olive oil, some acidic ingredient (vinegar or citrus juice), and flavorings (garlic, ginger, herbs, etc.). According to the food police, the proper ratio of oil to acid in salad dressings is 3 to 1. I won't deny that it works that way, but it adds so many calories and so much fat (albeit healthy fat) that I've altered that ratio a bit. Many of the recipes in this book specify a 2 to 1 ratio, some even 1 to 1. We need *some* oil as it gives a luxurious mouth feel to the salads and helps the dressing stick to the salad ingredients, but a little bit will do. With less oil, you can eat more salad and get more nutrients for the same number of calories. The Italians would call this getting *capre e cavoli* (goats *and* cabbages), the equivalent of having your cake and eating it too.

As far as making the dressings, if you're feeling lazy you can usually get away with just drizzling the oil, vinegar or citrus juice, and flavorings over top of the salad and mixing, although they can separate easily if not combined beforehand. You can whisk the ingredients vigorously in a bowl for 30 seconds or so, but if you have a jam jar and tight-fitting lid, you can just combine the ingredients and shake enthusiastically for about 10 seconds. It's quicker, with less mess and easier cleanup: *capre e cavoli* again!

1

# BEANS

Many of the recipes in this book contain some type of bean (or lentils, chickpeas, or other legume). In the recipes, I have specified the quantity of cooked beans to add, and these can come from a can (drained and rinsed) or you can cook them yourself. I usually use canned beans because they are always perfectly and uniformly cooked, firm but tender, and oh so easy. If you want to cook your own dry beans, soak them overnight in plenty of water and then rinse before cooking (lentils don't require soaking). Add the uncooked beans to a pot with a crushed garlic clove, a bay leaf, and enough cold water to cover the beans by about 2 inches. Adding salt will lengthen the cooking time but result in more flavorful beans that hold their shape better, so a good compromise would be to add just a bit. Bring to a boil, reduce the heat to a simmer, and cover. Check every 10 or 15 minutes to ensure that you have a nice lazy simmer going, to skim off any foam that develops, and to stir. Depending on the type and age of the beans, they usually take a bit over an hour to cook, but it can be longer for larger or older beans.

# FRESH, LOCAL, BLAH BLAH BLAH

You've heard it a million times: use the freshest, highest quality ingredients you can find (local, organic, vine-ripened, hand-picked, free trade, fair trade, unisex, wash-n-wear, nonstick, and of course, carbon neutral). I'm repeating that advice here not to insult your intelligence but because the quality and flavor of the individual ingredients is much more important in salads than it is in sauces or soups or other dishes. Raw ingredients have nowhere to hide and no time to develop flavors through long, slow cooking processes. For example, we've all had good tomatoes (sweet, tangy, juicy) and bad tomatoes (bland, mealy, flavorless), and you can imagine a salad made from each sort. 'Nuff said.

# HOW TO USE THIS BOOK

As with the *Accidentally Vegan Italian Soups* book, I've organized the salad recipes into three groups based on the level of difficulty and time required to make them. We start with the *Facilissimo* section (Very easy). These salads often require only opening a can or two of beans, adding some sun-dried tomatoes, olives, capers, or herbs, and chopping a couple of vegetables. The next section is *Facile* (Easy). These salads might require a larger number of ingredients, or one or two ingredients that take some extra preparation (e.g., cooking rice or roasting pumpkin). Salads that are *Un Po' Più Difficile* (A bit more difficult) could require a somewhat long ingredient list or multiple ingredients that require more extensive prep work (like making, chilling, and then frying polenta). I've also included a bonus section of three salads because they are not strictly Italian (such as the Caesar salad), not strictly accidentally vegan (e.g., contain vegan parmesan cheese), or include a difficult to find ingredient (e.g., fresh fava beans). But, they are three of my favorite vegan salads and too good to exclude based on these technicalities.

In the interest of making the best salads possible given the produce available to you at any given time, here is a brief list of the salads you might try when a few key ingredients are at their peak (either in your own garden or at the market or grocery store):

### Tomatoes
- *Insalata di Fagiolini alla Calabrese* (Calabrian Green Bean Salad)
- *Insalata di Pomodori* (Tomato Salad)
- *Insalata di Sedano e Cannellini* (Celery and Cannellini Bean Salad)
- *Insalata di Farro con Cannellini* (Farro and Cannellini Bean Salad)
- *Insalata Pantesca* (Potato and Tomato Salad)
- *Insalata alla Palermitana* (Palermo Salad)
- *Insalata di Riso alla Ligure* (Ligurian Rice Salad)
- *Insalata alla Polentona* (Fried Polenta Salad)

### Green beans
- *Insalata di Fagiolini alla Calabrese* (Calabrian Green Bean Salad)
- *Insalata alla Palermitana* (Palermo Salad)
- *Insalata di Riso alla Ligure* (Ligurian Rice Salad)

### Apples and pears
- *Insalata Mista Croccante* (Crunchy Mixed Salad)
- *Insalata di Cavolo Rosso e Mele* (Red Cabbage and Apple Salad)
- *Insalata di Riso Venere* (Black Venus Rice Salad)
- *Insalata d'Autunno* (Fall Salad)

- *Insalata di Radicchio e Pere* (Pear and Radicchio Salad)

## Zucchini
- *Insalata di Orzo e Zucchine* (Barley and Zucchini Salad)
- *Insalata Mista Croccante* (Crunchy Mixed Salad)
- *Insalata di Farro con Cannellini* (Farro and Cannellini Bean Salad)

## Oranges
- *Insalata Dolce d'Arancia* (Sweet Orange Salad)
- *Insalata d'Arancia* (Orange Salad)
- *Insalata di Foglie Amare e Arance* (Bitter Greens and Orange Salad)
- *Insalata di Lenticchie e Arance* (Lentil and Orange Salad)

## Pumpkins/squashes
- *Insalata d'Autunno* (Fall Salad)
- *Insalata di Fagioli Misti e Zucca* (Mixed Bean and Pumpkin Salad)

## Fennel
- *Insalata Dolce d'Arancia* (Sweet Orange Salad)
- *Insalata di Finocchio e Castagne* (Fennel and Chestnut Salad)
- *Insalata di Cavolo Cappuccio* (Cabbage Salad)
- *Insalata di Lenticchie e Arance* (Lentil and Orange Salad)

## Radicchio
- *Insalata di Foglie Amare e Arance* (Bitter Greens and Orange Salad)
- *Insalata di Radicchio e Pere* (Pear and Radicchio Salad)
- *Insalata di Radicchio alla Griglia* (Grilled Radicchio Salad)

## Grapes
- *Insalata di Cavolo Cappuccio* (Cabbage Salad)
- *Insalata di Lenticchie e Uva* (Lentil and Grape Salad)

# MAKE IT YOUR OWN

One of the tenets of Italian cuisine is that recipes are used as mere suggestions, hypothetical or prototypical ways to create a dish, and the recipes in this book are no exception. Prefer almonds to walnuts? By all means make that substitution. Have only apple cider vinegar when a recipe calls for the white wine variety? Give it a go. Love pine nuts? Double up. You may create something wonderful and at the very least it will be more suitable to your personal tastes. The same goes for my directions regarding salt and pepper. Different palates require different quantities, so it is always a good idea to combine all of the ingredients and then do a taste test before adding salt and pepper *a piacere* (a pleasing amount) or *quanto basta* (as much as is enough). That said, I have found that some of the main ingredients in this book (beans, potatoes, lentils, and raw vegetables) require significant salt for the flavors to really come alive.

The Italians say *mangiare per vivere e non vivere per mangiare* which means eat to live but don't live to eat. Or, as my grandmother used to say as I reached for my third piece of Easter bread or sixth anise pizzelle, you have to eat food that likes you, not just food that you like. With the recipes in this book we can have it both ways with nutritious, fortifying foods that are also a pleasure to eat. *Capre e cavoli.*

*Buon appetito!*

# FACILISSIMO
# (VERY EASY)

These salads are so easy! Open a can or two, drain a few olives or capers or sun-dried tomatoes, chop an onion, whisk up some olive oil and vinegar, and enjoy.

# INSALATA DOLCE D'ARANCIA
## (SWEET ORANGE SALAD)

Perhaps the most useful technique I learned in cooking school was how to make orange supremes (Sorry Chef Tom, I know that roux was important too). Supremes (or sections or segments) are a much more pleasant way to present and consume oranges in salads than merely chopping up a peeled orange. It will make you feel like a Roman emperor eating peeled grapes or the first person to eat seedless watermelon. To make supremes, first cut the base and top off the orange so that it will rest on the cutting board. Then, taking your sharpest small knife, cut off the peel right down to the orange flesh using curved motions from top to bottom. Repeat this around the orange then turn it upside down and, if you didn't perform the first set of cuts perfectly (I'm sure you did although I never do), clean up any remaining pith. Next, take the orange in hand and insert your knife along both edges of a section and remove the orange flesh (see the first page of the *Facilissimo* section of this book for a photo). Repeat around the entire orange. You can eat what is left over or squeeze it for a few precious sips of fresh orange juice.

### INGREDIENTS (2 MEALS OR 6 SIDES)

4 fennel bulbs, stalks, root ends, and outer leaves removed, sliced very thinly (about 20 ounces)
4 oranges, supremed
½ cup toasted pine nuts
½ cup raisins
¼ cup pumpkin seeds
3 tablespoons olive oil
2 tablespoons apple cider vinegar
Salt and pepper to taste

### PROCEDURES

**1.** Combine the fennel, orange supremes, pine nuts, raisins, and pumpkin seeds in a bowl and mix well.
**2.** Make the dressing by whisking together the olive oil and apple cider vinegar.
**3.** Drizzle the dressing over the salad, mix well, taste, and add salt and pepper as desired.

**4.** Take a few moments to decide whether you will be humble or loud and proud when the accolades start rolling in for this salad.

# INSALATA DI FINOCCHIO E CASTAGNE (FENNEL AND CHESTNUT SALAD)

Chestnuts can be difficult to find and difficult to prepare, despite the romantic notion of chestnuts roasting on an open fire as Jack Frost nips at our noses. In fact, in my town I can only find them a week or so before Christmas, and they are often none too fresh. For this salad (and almost any time I need chestnuts for a recipe) I like to order the snack-sized vacuum packs of roasted, peeled chestnuts available online or at specialty grocers. They are perfectly roasted and already peeled, sweet, moist, and delicious. The flavor profile of this salad is complex, with several very distinct flavors including fennel, chestnuts, ginger, and pine nuts. If preparing ahead of time (recommended!) you can leave out the greens and mix them in just before eating.

## INGREDIENTS (2 MEALS OR 6 SIDES)

2 fennel bulbs, stalks, root ends, and outer leaves removed, sliced very thinly (about 10 ounces)
6 ounces (about 1 cup) prepared chestnuts, roughly chopped or sliced
4 ounces baby greens (or field greens)
2 tablespoons olive oil
Juice of 1 lime
½ tablespoon grated ginger
Salt and pepper to taste
¼ cup toasted pine nuts
2 green onions, sliced thinly

## PROCEDURES

**1.** Combine the fennel, chestnuts, and baby greens in a bowl and mix well.
**2.** Make the dressing by whisking together the olive oil, lime juice, and grated ginger.
**3.** Drizzle the dressing over the salad, mix well, taste, and add salt and pepper as desired.
**4.** Garnish with pine nuts and green onions.

# INSALATA DI FAGIOLINI ALLA CALABRESE
## (CALABRIAN GREEN BEAN SALAD)

Leave it to the Calabrians to take the humble green bean and create a delicious, healthy, light salad. If possible, you should use fresh green beans in early summer (from your garden or a farmer's market), but even frozen green beans work well in this recipe. Heck, you can even use canned green beans (in cases of culinary emergency or post-apocalyptic famine); just drain them and skip the first step below. However, if you are an aficionado of fresh green beans this salad presents a perfect excuse to sit in a rocking chair on the front porch snapping the tips off these garden treasures.

## INGREDIENTS (2 MEALS OR 6 SIDES)

1 pound green beans (tips removed), cut into 1" pieces
20 cherry or grape tomatoes, halved
½ cup black olives, pitted and sliced
2 tablespoons olive oil
3 tablespoons white wine vinegar
2 garlic cloves, peeled and minced
1 tablespoon dried oregano
¼ teaspoon crushed red pepper
Salt and pepper to taste

## PROCEDURES

**1.** Boil the green beans in salted water until tender, about 5-7 minutes depending on thickness. Drain and rinse with cold tap water. Allow them to dry well so that they can absorb the oil and vinegar.

**2.** Combine the green beans, tomatoes, and olives in a bowl and mix well.

**3.** Make the dressing by whisking together the olive oil, vinegar, garlic, oregano, and crushed red pepper.

**4.** Drizzle the dressing over the salad, mix well, taste, and add salt and pepper as desired.

# INSALATA DI CANNELLINI
# (CANNELLINI BEAN SALAD)

I almost reserved this recipe for the upcoming *Accidentally Vegan Italian Companatici* book (loosely translated as "things you put on top of bread" or simply "accompaniments" with the existence of bread on the Italian table being assumed). But this salad is so delicious and easy that I could not help but include it here. The flavor of this salad is intense and so it may be better as a side salad than a meal in itself unless you are in a mood to have your taste buds overloaded (as I often am).

## INGREDIENTS (2 MEALS OR 6 SIDES)

3 cups cooked cannellini beans (or two 15-ounce cans, drained and rinsed)
8 sun-dried tomatoes in oil, drained and chopped
½ red onion, peeled and sliced thinly
½ cup green olives, pitted and sliced
2 tablespoons capers, drained
3 tablespoons olive oil
Juice of ½ lemon
Salt and pepper to taste
1 tablespoon chopped parsley

## PROCEDURES

**1.** Combine the beans, sun-dried tomatoes, onions, olives, and capers in a bowl and mix well.
**2.** Make the dressing by whisking together the olive oil and lemon juice.
**3.** Drizzle the dressing over the salad, mix well, taste, and add salt and pepper as desired.
**4.** Top with chopped parsley while contemplating the notion that the simple things in life are the best.

# PANZANELLA
## (TOMATO AND BREAD SALAD)

Rumor has it that no self-respecting cook would add anything other than bread, tomatoes, basil, salt, oil, and vinegar to panzanella. Those of us with more modest levels of self-esteem are free to do as we please, although I've only gone a bit further by adding red onion, two vinegars, and pepper. Other versions of this salad also include celery, cucumber, bell peppers, and capers, so feel free to experiment. I like this simpler version, however, so as to not hide the juicy, salty, carby main point of this salad: tomatoes and bread. Having a slightly stale loaf on the counter is a good motivation to make this salad. The bread can be torn and left to dry for a few hours or dried a bit in a 300-degree oven for 10-15 minutes so that it will soak up the juice from the tomatoes. This is the perfect make-ahead salad as it will be much better after a night in the refrigerator. I would also recommend the juiciest tomatoes you can find (probably not Roma), and don't leave that juice on the cutting board!

## INGREDIENTS (2 MEALS OR 6 SIDES)

6 slices of rustic bread (about 8 ounces), torn into bite-sized pieces.
2 pounds mixed tomatoes, diced
½ red onion, peeled and sliced thinly
10 basil leaves, torn or roughly chopped
3 tablespoons olive oil
1 tablespoon red wine vinegar
1 teaspoon balsamic vinegar
Salt and pepper to taste

## PROCEDURES

**1.** Combine the torn bread, tomatoes, onion, basil, and a big pinch of salt in a bowl and mix well.
**2.** Make the dressing by whisking together the olive oil, red wine vinegar, and balsamic vinegar.
**3.** Drizzle the dressing over the salad, mix well, and place in the refrigerator (for at least a couple of hours; overnight is better).
**4.** Taste and add salt and pepper as desired.

# INSALATA MISTA CROCCANTE (CRUNCHY MIXED SALAD)

I love tart apples such as Granny Smith in this salad. The combination of apples and apple cider vinegar is the main flavor dimension, accented by the mustard and pine nuts, sweetened by the carrots. Yummers. If you make this salad ahead of time (a good idea to let the flavors meld together), keep the baby greens separate and mix them in just before service. You can toast the pine nuts in a dry frying pan over medium heat for about 4-5 minutes, shaking very frequently. Chopping the carrots, zucchini, celery, and apples into a size-matched small dice makes for a nice presentation and gives you a bit of each flavor along with plenty of crunch in every bite. Denture wearers, *uomo avvisato, mezzo salvato!* (one who is warned is half saved!).

## INGREDIENTS (2 MEALS OR 6 SIDES)

2 carrots, peeled and diced small
1 medium zucchini (unpeeled but seeded), diced small
1 celery stalk, diced small
2 apples, cored and diced small
3 ounces baby greens (or field greens)
2 tablespoons olive oil
2 tablespoons apple cider vinegar
2 tablespoons stone ground mustard
Salt and pepper to taste
¼ cup toasted pine nuts

## PROCEDURES

**1.** Combine the carrots, zucchini, celery, apple, and baby greens in a bowl and mix well.
**2.** Make the dressing by whisking together the olive oil, vinegar, and mustard.
**3.** Drizzle the dressing over the salad, mix well, taste, and add salt and pepper as desired.
**4.** Garnish with the pine nuts.

# INSALATA D'ARANCIA
## (ORANGE SALAD)

This salad is a great contrast to the Sweet Orange Salad (*Insalata Dolce d'Arancia*) and you would hardly guess that they are based on the same fruit because their flavors are so different. This salad is savory with an accent of sweetness, the other is sweet with an accent of savory. In reality, Italians would usually just refer to each of these as an orange salad. These salads are especially popular in Sicily where many oranges are grown and consumed to escape from the summer heat.

### INGREDIENTS (2 MEALS OR 6 SIDES)

6 oranges, supremed (see *Insalata Dolce d'Arancia* recipe for instructions and the first page of the *Facilissimo* section of this book for a photo)
½ red onion, peeled and sliced thinly
½ cup green olives, pitted and sliced
½ cup black olives, pitted and sliced
10 basil leaves, roughly chopped
2 tablespoons olive oil
Salt and pepper to taste

### PROCEDURES

**1.** Combine the orange supremes, onion, olives, and basil in a bowl and mix well.

**2.** Drizzle the olive oil over the salad, mix well, taste, and add salt and pepper as desired.

**3.** Try not to be too hard on yourself for eating plain oranges by themselves all these years before you knew how they could come alive with a few simple additions. We all make mistakes.

# INSALATA DI CAVOLO CAPPUCCIO
## (CABBAGE SALAD)

*Cavolo* (cabbage) abounds in Italy, and there are many different types. Cabbage has made its way into Italian culture in phrases such as *fatti i cavoli tuoi* (literally, "you do your own cabbages" and figuratively "mind your own darn business!"). I mean really, why don't you mind your own cabbages and leave my cabbages to me? You can also just exclaim *cavolo!* in place of dang or darn it or wow! In any case, this salad uses regular green cabbage (called *cappuccio*, no relation to *cappuccino* despite what my spell checker thinks) along with red cabbage and fennel for a triple dose of healthy earthiness.

## INGREDIENTS (2 MEALS OR 6 SIDES)

¼ head green cabbage, cored and chopped or sliced thinly (about 6 ounces)
¼ head red cabbage, cored and chopped or sliced thinly (about 6 ounces)
1 fennel bulb, stalk, root end, and outer leaves removed, sliced very thinly (about 5 ounces)
8 ounces green grapes, sliced
8 ounces red grapes, sliced
2 tablespoons olive oil
Juice of 1 lemon
1 tablespoon ground mustard
Salt and pepper to taste
½ cup walnuts, chopped and toasted

## PROCEDURES

**1.** Combine the cabbage, fennel, and grapes in a bowl and mix well.
**2.** Make the dressing by whisking together the olive oil, lemon juice, and mustard.
**3.** Drizzle the dressing over the salad, mix well, taste, and add salt and pepper as desired.
**4.** Garnish with walnuts.

# INSALATA DI FOGLIE AMARE E ARANCE
## (BITTER GREENS AND ORANGE SALAD)

If you like sweet salads, there are plenty of oranges and golden raisins to keep your sweet tooth happy here. Or, perhaps you prefer salads with some earthy bitterness? Then you'll surely enjoy the savory arugula and radicchio. The magic of this salad is the perfectly balanced sweetness and bitterness that gives a unique flavor. Topping with some toasty pine nuts (sweet and bitter atop sweetness and bitterness) brings it all home.

## INGREDIENTS (2 MEALS OR 6 SIDES)

2 oranges, supremed (see *Insalata Dolce d'Arancia* recipe for instructions and the first page of the *Facilissimo* section of this book for a photo), juice retained
¼ cup golden raisins
3 ounces baby arugula
½ medium-sized radicchio head, cored and sliced thinly (about 4 ounces prepared)
2 tablespoons olive oil
Salt and pepper to taste
¼ cup toasted pine nuts

## PROCEDURES

**1.** Combine the orange supremes, golden raisins, arugula, and radicchio in a bowl and mix well.
**2.** Make the dressing by squeezing the juice from the orange portion remaining after the wedges have been removed and whisking the juice with the olive oil.
**3.** Drizzle the dressing over the salad, mix well, taste, and add salt and pepper as desired.
**4.** Garnish with the pine nuts.

# INSALATA DI CECI
## (CHICKPEA SALAD)

Italians love their *ceci* (che-chee) and have found a way to eat them in sandwiches, desserts, soups, and of course, salads. This salad is savory, tangy, filling, and perfect for your laziest mood. If you use jarred and julienned sun-dried tomatoes, canned chickpeas, and canned, sliced olives, this salad can be made about as quickly as you can slice an onion.

## INGREDIENTS (2 MEALS OR 6 SIDES)

1½ cups cooked chickpeas (or one 15-ounce can, drained and rinsed)
5 sun-dried tomatoes in oil, drained and chopped
3 ounces baby greens (or field greens)
¼ cup green olives, pitted and sliced
¼ cup black olives, pitted and sliced
½ red onion, peeled and sliced thinly
2 tablespoons olive oil
Juice of ½ lemon
1 tablespoon dried oregano
Salt and pepper to taste

## PROCEDURES

**1.** Combine the chickpeas, sun-dried tomatoes, greens, olives, and onion in a bowl and mix well.
**2.** Make the dressing by whisking together the olive oil, lemon juice, and oregano.
**3.** Drizzle the dressing over the salad, mix well, taste, and add salt and pepper as desired.

# INSALATA DI CAVOLO ROSSO E MELE (RED CABBAGE AND APPLE SALAD)

I like nice big chunks of almond in this recipe, so when I indicate "slivered or chopped" for the almonds below, my advice is to merely pass the knife over the almonds as if giving a blessing or just trying to frighten them a bit. That may be an exaggeration, but when apple and cabbage meet a big chunk of almond in a single bite, contentment ensues. I've even doubled the quantity of almonds often seen in this type of salad to better balance these three flavors. *Cavolo!*

## INGREDIENTS (2 MEALS OR 6 SIDES)

1 head red cabbage, quartered, cored, and sliced thinly
1 carrot, peeled and grated
2 apples, cored and diced
3 tablespoons olive oil
3 tablespoons apple cider vinegar
Salt and pepper to taste
½ cup almonds, slivered or chopped and toasted

## PROCEDURES

**1.** Combine the cabbage, carrot, and apple pieces in a bowl and mix well.
**2.** Make the dressing by whisking together the olive oil and apple cider vinegar.
**3.** Drizzle the dressing over the salad, mix well, taste, and add salt and pepper as desired.
**4.** Garnish with the almonds.

# INSALATA DI POMODORI (TOMATO SALAD)

Well, you knew it was coming. No book of Italian salads would be complete without a big, juicy, sweet, salty pile of *pomodori*. Having a variety of tomatoes in this salad accentuates the complexity of this delightful vegetable fruit. I've specified cherry or grape, plum, and regular tomatoes, but any varieties will do and there are more and more heirloom tomatoes showing up at farmers markets and even grocery stores these days. Using some yellow or dark tomatoes can also add to the beauty of this salad and provide different textures and flavors. No napkins allowed because you can't say that you fully enjoyed this salad without tomato juice running down your chin.

## INGREDIENTS (2 MEALS OR 6 SIDES)

1½ pounds of mixed tomatoes (cherry, grape, red, yellow, etc.) cut into bite-sized chunks
5 basil leaves, roughly chopped
1 teaspoon dried oregano
2 tablespoons olive oil
1 tablespoon balsamic vinegar
Salt and pepper to taste

## PROCEDURES

**1.** Combine the tomatoes and basil in a bowl and mix well.
**2.** Make the dressing by whisking together the oregano, olive oil, and balsamic vinegar.
**3.** Drizzle the dressing over the salad, mix well, taste, and add salt and pepper as desired.
**4.** Enjoy!

# INSALATA DI FAGIOLI E CIPOLLA (BEAN AND ONION SALAD)

If you use canned beans you can make this salad in about 5 minutes, the time it takes to chop an onion and tear some bread. However, letting the salad either sit at room temperature for an hour or so or refrigerating overnight and then letting it come back to room temperature before eating allows the bread and beans to be infused with the oniony goodness. It's a reminder of how satisfying simple dishes can be, and makes me think that the more elaborate, "sophisticated," and complicated recipes in the world are missing a crucial point. Of course, you should use some delicious, rustic, crusty, yeasty bread for this salad.

## INGREDIENTS (2 MEALS OR 6 SIDES)

3 cups cooked cannellini beans (or two 15-ounce cans, drained and rinsed)
½ red onion, peeled and sliced thinly
2 slices rustic white bread, torn into bite-sized pieces
3 tablespoons olive oil
Salt and pepper to taste
2 tablespoons chopped parsley

## PROCEDURES

**1.** Combine the beans, onion, and bread in a bowl and mix well.
**2.** Drizzle the olive oil over the salad, mix well, taste, and add salt and pepper as desired.
**3.** Top with the chopped parsley and enjoy!

# INSALATA DI SEDANO E CANNELLINI
## (CELERY AND CANNELLINI BEAN SALAD)

Step into the spotlight celery, no more playing second fiddle to potatoes, onions, or carrots. Celery is rarely the leading lady, with the exception of this salad. When picking out a bunch of celery for this recipe, try to find one with as many tender green leaves in the center as you can, and use them all. This is one of the simplest salads in this book, and maybe it takes a short ingredient list for celery to shine through. Remember that the main ingredients in this salad (celery, cannellini beans, and tomatoes) *love* salt, so at least for this salad do not hold back.

## INGREDIENTS (2 MEALS OR 6 SIDES)

3 cups cooked cannellini beans (or two 15-ounce cans, drained and rinsed)
20 cherry tomatoes, halved
4 celery stalks and their green leaves, diced
3 tablespoons olive oil
Salt and pepper to taste

## PROCEDURES

**1.** Combine the beans, tomatoes, and celery in a bowl and mix well.
**2.** Drizzle the olive oil over the salad, mix well, taste, and add salt and pepper as desired.
**3.** Think about whether you know any human equivalents of celery...someone who usually hides in the background but could truly shine if given the chance.

# FACILE
# (EASY)

A bit more complicated, these salads might require slicing a mango, cooking a few potatoes or some rice, or chopping more than a few vegetables. But they are still easy, so get to it!

# INSALATA DI RADICCHIO E PERE (PEAR AND RADICCHIO SALAD)

Italians call someone who falls in love quickly one who *cascare come una pera matura* (literally, falls like a ripe pear). Well, I have fallen for this salad in precisely this way, landing with a distinctive *ker-thump* on the kitchen floor. I never realized there were so many different kinds of crunchy until having this salad. The radicchio, the pear, the walnuts, the fried breadcrumbs, they are all crunchy in their own distinctive way, and it's possible that your neighbors will hear you eating this dish if your walls are thin. The more bitter the radicchio and the sweeter the pear, the more profound the contrast and better this salad will be.

## INGREDIENTS (2 MEALS OR 6 SIDES)

2 medium-sized radicchio heads, halved, cored, and sliced thinly (about 1 pound prepared)
2 green pears, cored and diced
¼ cup walnuts, chopped and toasted
4 tablespoons olive oil (divided 2 + 2)
1 tablespoon balsamic vinegar
1 tablespoon stone ground mustard
Salt and pepper to taste
2 slices of your favorite bread, torn into pieces
1 teaspoon dried oregano
¼ teaspoon crushed red pepper

## PROCEDURES

**1.** Combine the radicchio, pear, and walnuts in a bowl and mix well.
**2.** Make the dressing by whisking together the first 2 tablespoons of oil, the vinegar, and the mustard.
**3.** Drizzle the dressing over the salad, mix well, taste and add salt and pepper as desired.
**4.** Combine the bread pieces, oregano, and crushed red pepper in a food processor and blend for 1-2 minutes until no large pieces remain (but before it resembles cornmeal).
**5.** Fry the aromatic breadcrumbs with the remaining 2 tablespoons of olive oil over medium heat for approximately 4-5 minutes, stirring frequently. Pay extra attention near the end as they go from not done to

overdone very quickly. (It's better to remove them from the heat a bit early, as they'll continue to brown a bit).

**6.** If not serving immediately, keep the breadcrumbs and salad separate until ready to eat. The breadcrumbs can be kept for a few days, covered, at room temperature.

# INSALATA DI ORZO E ZUCCHINE (BARLEY AND ZUCCHINI SALAD)

Zucchini and barley (in Italian, *orzo* is barley) are a classic combination in Italy. I suspect that Italians, like Americans, are faced with the "problem" in late summer of an overabundance of zucchini, growing larger and tougher by the day. With this recipe in hand, we can finally start saying yes when our neighbors offer to pay us to take their zucchini. After preparation, this salad benefits from resting overnight in the refrigerator and then being left on the counter for an hour or so to come up to room temperature before eating. The main ingredients in this salad require significant salt to come to life, so don't scrimp.

## INGREDIENTS (2 MEALS OR 6 SIDES)

1 cup uncooked pearled barley
2 medium zucchinis (unpeeled but seeded), grated
1 carrot, peeled and grated
10 basil leaves, roughly chopped
3 tablespoons olive oil
3 tablespoons white wine vinegar
2 garlic cloves, peeled and minced
Salt and pepper to taste
¼ cup almonds, slivered or chopped and toasted

## PROCEDURES

**1.** Bring a pot of water (about 1 quart) to a boil and add a teaspoon of salt. Stir in the barley, return to a simmer and cover, adjusting the heat so that it is barely simmering. Cook for 30 minutes (until the barley is tender but not mushy). Drain and rinse with cold tap water.

**2.** Place the grated zucchini in a dishtowel and squeeze firmly and repeatedly over the sink to remove the excess water.

**3.** Combine the barley, zucchini, carrot, and basil in a bowl and mix well.

**4.** Make the dressing by whisking together the olive oil, white wine vinegar, and minced garlic.

**5.** Drizzle the dressing over the salad, mix well, taste, and add salt and pepper as desired.

**6.** For best results, allow the flavors to blend for an hour at room temperature or, even better, overnight in the refrigerator.

**7.** Top with the almonds.

# INSALATA DI FARRO CON CANNELLINI
## (FARRO AND CANNELLINI BEAN SALAD)

Don't confuse cannellini beans with other white beans, large or small. The defining property of cannellini beans is a texture that somehow manages to be firm and creamy at the same time. You *could* substitute navy beans or great northern beans in recipes calling for cannellini beans, in the same way that you *could* substitute watching a Sofia Loren movie for a trip to Italy, but as in the latter case you'll notice the difference. Cannellini beans are a type of kidney bean and despite the fact that they are native to South America, they were adopted by Italians as soon as they had the chance. Who could blame them?

## INGREDIENTS (2 MEALS OR 6 SIDES)

1 cup uncooked farro
10 cherry or grape tomatoes, halved
1 medium zucchini (unpeeled), quartered lengthwise, seeds removed, and sliced thinly
1½ cups cooked cannellini beans (or one 15-ounce can, drained and rinsed)
10 basil leaves, roughly chopped
½ cup green olives, pitted
3 tablespoons olive oil
Salt and pepper to taste

## PROCEDURES

**1.** Bring a pot of water (about 1 quart) to a boil and add a teaspoon of salt. Stir in the farro, return to a simmer and cover, adjusting the heat so that it is barely simmering. Cook for 30 minutes (until the farro is tender but not mushy). Drain and rinse with cold tap water.

**2.** Combine the farro, tomatoes, zucchini, and beans in a bowl and mix well.

**3.** Make the dressing by adding the basil, olives, and olive oil to a food processor and blending well. The dressing will be thick, but you can add a bit more olive oil if you like.

**4.** Spoon the dressing over the salad, mix well, taste, and add salt and pepper as desired.

**5.** Eat immediately or refrigerate (better) for 1 hour to 1 day.

# PATATE PREZZEMOLATE
## (ITALIAN POTATO SALAD)

After eating this salad, you'll wonder why Americans cover their potatoes in mayonnaise and why the French douse them in vinegar. You might prefer to leave the skins on, although I can still remember my grandfather wondering why we eat potato skins in America while as a poor boy in Italy he was told to throw them to the pigs. You can use new potatoes in this recipe. If they are quite small, you can boil them whole with their skins on and then rub off the skin easily after they cool a bit, cutting them in half if need be.

### INGREDIENTS (2 MEALS OR 6 SIDES)

1 tablespoon salt
1½ pounds red potatoes (about 6), peeled and cut into bite-sized pieces
3 tablespoons olive oil
2 garlic cloves, peeled and minced
3 tablespoons chopped chives
¼ teaspoon crushed red pepper
¼ cup chopped parsley
Salt and pepper to taste

### PROCEDURES

**1.** Add the salt to a large pot of water (at least 2 quarts), add the potatoes and bring to a boil.
**2.** Boil the potatoes for approximately 10-12 minutes, until a sharp knife inserted into a large piece of potato goes in and comes out with very little resistance (or take a piece out and see if it smashes easily with a fork). Drain but don't rinse the potatoes and place them in a bowl.
**3.** Make the dressing by whisking together the olive oil, minced garlic, chives, crushed red pepper, and chopped parsley.
**4.** Drizzle the dressing over the potatoes, mix well, taste, and add salt and pepper as desired.

# BORLOTTI IN INSALATA
## (BORLOTTI BEAN SALAD)

To create borlotti beans, Italians took cranberry beans and bred them to have thicker skins, I suspect to match their personalities. Borlotti beans can be purchased dry online or at some grocery stores (particularly Mediterranean and specialty grocers). Their thicker skins hide creamy, nutty flesh that goes perfectly with tangy additions like garlic and green onions. It is difficult to find fresh borlotti beans (unless you grow them yourself) or even canned versions, so for this recipe I am assuming that you will start with dry beans. That said, if you can find fresh ones this salad would be even better; just substitute 3 cups of fresh beans and cook them for only 30 minutes.

## INGREDIENTS (2 MEALS OR 6 SIDES)

1½ cups dry borlotti beans, soaked overnight
2 garlic cloves, smashed and peeled
1 bay leaf
5 sun-dried tomatoes in oil, drained and chopped
5 basil leaves, roughly chopped
2 tablespoons olive oil
1 tablespoon white wine vinegar
½ teaspoon dried thyme
Salt and pepper to taste
2 green onions, sliced thinly

## PROCEDURES

**1.** Drain and add the uncooked beans to a pot with about 6 cups of cold water, the peeled, smashed garlic cloves, 1 teaspoon of salt, and the bay leaf. Bring to a boil over medium heat, then reduce heat to a simmer and cover. Every 15 minutes, skim any foam that appears and stir. Simmer until the beans are tender but not mushy (usually a little over an hour for dry beans that have been soaked overnight, although they can take longer). Drain, remove the bay leaf and garlic, and allow to cool.

**2.** Combine the cooked beans, sun-dried tomatoes, and basil in a bowl and mix well.

**3.** Make the dressing by whisking together the olive oil, vinegar, and dried thyme.

**4.** Drizzle the dressing over the salad, mix well, taste, and add salt and pepper as desired.

**5.** Top with the sliced green onions.

# INSALATA PANTESCA
## (POTATO AND TOMATO SALAD)

This salad hails from the island of Pantelleria, which may hold the record for extravagant nicknames including *Daughter of the Wind* and *Black Pearl of the Mediterranean*. The island sits between Sicily and Tunisia, closer to the latter but administratively Italian. It is truly a place belonging to the entire world, with Greek, Roman, African, French, Italian, and American influences (the latter owing mostly to the use of Pantelleria as a base of operations in the fight for Sicily in World War II). This salad reflects that diversity with originally Greek capers, Italian olives, onions, and herbs, and potatoes and tomatoes from the New World.

## INGREDIENTS (2 MEALS OR 6 SIDES)

1 tablespoon salt
3 large Yukon Gold potatoes, peeled and diced
20 cherry tomatoes, halved
2 tablespoons capers, drained
¼ cup green olives, pitted and sliced
½ red onion, peeled and sliced thinly
3 tablespoons olive oil
1 tablespoon white wine vinegar
1 tablespoon dried oregano
Salt and pepper to taste
5 basil leaves, roughly chopped

## PROCEDURES

**1.** Add the salt to a large pot of water (at least 2 quarts), add the potatoes and bring to a boil.
**2.** Boil the potatoes for approximately 10-12 minutes, until a sharp knife inserted into a large piece of potato goes in and comes out with very little resistance (or take a piece out and see if it smashes easily with a fork). Drain but don't rinse the potatoes.
**3.** Combine the potatoes, tomatoes, capers, olives, and onion in a bowl and mix well.
**4.** Make the dressing by whisking together the olive oil, white wine vinegar, and oregano.

**5.** Drizzle the dressing over the salad, mix well, taste, and add salt and pepper as desired.

**6.** Garnish with the chopped basil.

# INSALATA ALLA PALERMITANA
## (PALERMO SALAD)

Known as *'Nzalata all'Antica* in Sicilian, this "antique salad" was created to make use of vegetables cooked by grocers to save families from having to start a wood fire inside their homes to cook vegetables during the unbearably hot Sicilian summers. Roasted peppers and boiled green beans were sold alongside the fresh tomatoes and onions for this salad. You can use canned green beans for this recipe instead of fresh beans. If you do, skip the steps for cooking them (and you'll only need one pot).

## INGREDIENTS (2 MEALS OR 6 SIDES)

1 tablespoon salt
2 large Yukon Gold potatoes, peeled and diced
12 ounces green beans (tips removed), cut into 1" pieces
1 cup roasted red bell peppers, chopped
4 tomatoes, diced
½ red onion, peeled and sliced thinly
5 basil leaves, roughly chopped
3 tablespoons olive oil
2 tablespoons red wine vinegar
Salt and pepper to taste

## PROCEDURES

**1.** Fill two pots with water (about 2 quarts each) and add ½ tablespoon of salt to each. In one pot, add the potatoes, and bring both pots to a boil.

**2.** Boil the potatoes for approximately 10-12 minutes, until a sharp knife inserted into a large piece of potato goes in and comes out with very little resistance (or take a piece out and see if it smashes easily with a fork). Drain but don't rinse the potatoes.

**3.** When the water in the second pot boils, add the green bean pieces and cook for approximately 5 minutes until tender but still firm. Drain but don't rinse the green beans.

**4.** Combine the potatoes, green beans, red bell peppers, tomatoes, onion, and basil in a bowl and mix well.

**5.** Make the dressing by whisking together the olive oil and red wine vinegar.

**6.** Drizzle the dressing over the salad, mix well, taste, and add salt and pepper as desired.

# INSALATA DI LENTICCHIE E UVA (LENTIL AND GRAPE SALAD)

If you find yourself trying to feed a stubborn lentil denier, even it if is yourself, this salad should do the trick. The sweet grapes along with the tangy ginger and garlic dress up the lentils in their Sunday-go-to-meetin' clothes. You might even forget they are there until you feel the surge of energy and happiness and good fortune that invariably accompanies the eating of lentils.

## INGREDIENTS (2 MEALS OR 6 SIDES)

1 cup dried brown or green lentils
2 garlic cloves, smashed and peeled
1 bay leaf
8 ounces green or red grapes (or 4 ounces of each), sliced
½ red onion, peeled and sliced thinly
½ cup walnuts, chopped and toasted
2 tablespoons olive oil
Juice of 1 lemon
1 teaspoon grated ginger
Salt and pepper to taste
1 tablespoon chopped parsley

## PROCEDURES

**1.** Add the lentils to a pot with 4 cups of cold water, the peeled, smashed garlic cloves, and the bay leaf. Bring to a boil over medium heat, then reduce heat to a simmer and cover. Simmer until the lentils are tender, about 25-30 minutes. Drain, remove the bay leaf and garlic, and allow to cool.

**2.** Combine the lentils, grapes, onion, and walnuts in a bowl and mix well.

**3.** Make the dressing by whisking together the olive oil, lemon juice, and ginger.

**4.** Drizzle the dressing over the salad, mix well, taste, and add salt and pepper as desired.

**5.** Garnish with the chopped parsley.

# INSALATA DI LENTICCHIE E ARANCE
# (LENTIL AND ORANGE SALAD)

A protein-packed twist on the traditional fennel and orange salad, this recipe turns a sweet treat into a proper meal with the addition of lentils. Lentils are eaten on New Year's Eve in Italy to bring prosperity in the new year, possibly because lentils resemble very small coins. Small, yes, but if you have enough of them the rewards are great, whether it is coins in your bank account or lentils in this salad.

## INGREDIENTS (2 MEALS OR 6 SIDES)

1 cup dried brown or green lentils
2 garlic cloves, smashed and peeled
1 bay leaf
2 oranges, supremed (see *Insalata Dolce d'Arancia* recipe for instructions and the first page of the *Facilissimo* section of this book for a photo), juice retained
2 green onions, sliced thinly
1 fennel bulb, stalk, root end, and outer leaves removed, sliced very thinly (about 5 ounces)
2 tablespoons olive oil
1 tablespoon balsamic vinegar
Salt and pepper to taste
½ cup walnuts, chopped and toasted

## PROCEDURES

**1.** Add the lentils to a pot with 4 cups of cold water, the peeled, smashed garlic cloves, and the bay leaf. Bring to a boil over medium heat, then reduce heat to a simmer and cover. Simmer until the lentils are tender, about 25-30 minutes. Drain, remove the bay leaf and garlic, and allow to cool.
**2.** Combine the lentils, orange supremes, green onions, and fennel in a bowl and mix well.
**3.** Make the dressing by whisking together the olive oil, balsamic vinegar, and juice from the orange husks.
**4.** Drizzle the dressing over the salad, mix well, taste, and add salt and pepper as desired.
**5.** Garnish with walnuts.

# INSALATA DI RISO ALLA LIGURE
# (LIGURIAN RICE SALAD)

This salad usually calls for the addition of pesto, and pesto often contains cheese (although there are many types that do not). For this recipe, we are resurrecting a 500-year-old Ligurian pesto that is heavy on the garlic. In fact, the name of this pesto, *agliata*, is based on the Italian word for garlic, *aglio*. Given the amount of garlic, this is a good salad to make when your significant other is out of town for a day (or two). I usually make twice the quantity of *agliata* needed for this salad because it is more amenable to the food processor, and the extra is great served on bread (the quantities specified below produce this double batch). The *agliata* can also be made in a small smoothie-type prep blender although, horror of horrors, you may have to add more olive oil.

## INGREDIENTS (2 MEALS OR 6 SIDES)

1 cup rice (Italian short grain like Arborio or Carnaroli are great)
6 ounces green beans (tips removed), cut into 1" pieces
½ red onion, peeled and sliced thinly
8 sun-dried tomatoes in oil, drained and chopped
½ cup black olives, pitted and sliced
4 tablespoons olive oil
1 tablespoon white wine vinegar
½ cup walnuts, chopped and toasted
6 garlic cloves, smashed and peeled
10 basil leaves, roughly chopped
Salt and pepper to taste

## PROCEDURES

**1.** Add the rice to 2 cups of water with a half teaspoon of salt in a small pot. Place over medium heat and bring to a simmer, then reduce the heat and cover. After a minute or two, check that the water is simmering but not boiling furiously. Cover and cook without stirring for 20 minutes. Check that all the liquid has been absorbed. If not, continue cooking for a few more minutes until the rice has absorbed all the water. Remove from heat and let cool.

**2.** Boil the green beans in a pot of boiling, salted water for 5 minutes. Drain and rinse with cold water.

**3.** Combine the rice, green beans, onion, sun-dried tomatoes, and olives in a bowl and mix well. Taste and add salt and pepper as desired.

**4.** Make the *agliata* by combining the olive oil, white wine vinegar, walnuts, garlic, and basil in a food processor and blending for 1-2 minutes, scraping down the sides as necessary, until you have a dressing with no pea-sized pieces remaining (but it should be textured and a bit chunky).

**5.** Spoon the *agliata* over the top and serve (to yourself and anyone else you won't be kissing).

# INSALATA DI RISO VENERE
# (BLACK VENUS RICE SALAD)

*Riso Venere*, rice of Venus, is a black rice originally derived by combining Chinese black rice with white Italian rice. The most notable characteristic of this rice is the aroma as it cooks, and the flavor of this aroma (if I may write such a strange phrase) when eaten. It is floral but not flowery, sweet but not sugary. Don't rinse this rice after cooking because the beautiful purple color staining all the other ingredients adds some elegance to the final presentation.

## INGREDIENTS (2 MEALS OR 6 SIDES)

4 tablespoons olive oil (divided 2 + 2)
½ yellow or white onion, peeled and diced
Leaves from 1 sprig of rosemary, roughly chopped
½ teaspoon dried oregano
1 cup black rice (*Riso Venere* or forbidden rice)
1 cup fresh or frozen sweet peas
1 red bell pepper, diced
1 yellow bell pepper, diced
1 apple, cored and diced
1 carrot, peeled and grated or diced small
Juice of 1 lemon
Salt and pepper to taste

## PROCEDURES

**1.** Fry the onion with the rosemary and oregano in 2 tablespoons of olive oil over medium heat for 5 minutes. Add the uncooked rice and mix well. Add 2 cups of water, bring to a simmer, reduce the heat to low and cover. After a minute or two, check that the water is simmering but not boiling furiously. Cover and cook without stirring for 30 minutes. Check that all the liquid has been absorbed. If not, continue cooking for 5-10 additional minutes until the rice has absorbed all the liquid. Remove from heat and let cool.

**2.** Boil the peas in a pot of boiling, salted water for 5 minutes. Drain and rinse with cold water.

**3.** Combine the rice, peas, bell pepper, apple, and carrot in a bowl and mix well.

**4.** Make the dressing by whisking together the remaining 2 tablespoons of olive oil and lemon juice.

**5.** Drizzle the dressing over the salad, mix well, taste, and add salt and pepper as desired.

**6.** Decide if you want to eat this salad or have it varnished to use as a table centerpiece for years to come, like an expensive and realistic bowl of plastic fruit.

# INSALATA DI CAVOLFIORE ROMANESCO
## (ROMANESCO SALAD)

The quantities for the Romanesco and the broccoli in this recipe are given for the cleaned florets because there is so much variation in how much stalk comes with the florets from store to store. For both the Romanesco and the broccoli, you'll need about 8 ounces of cleaned florets, which is usually half the weight of the whole crowns as purchased (so figure on about one pound of each type from the store). Romanesco's fractal appearance gives this salad a certain accidental sophistication.

## INGREDIENTS (2 MEALS OR 6 SIDES)

8 ounces Romanesco florets
8 ounces broccoli florets
1 tablespoon salt
¼ cup green olives, pitted and sliced
¼ cup black olives, pitted and sliced
½ cup roasted red bell peppers, chopped
3 tablespoons olive oil
Juice of 1 lemon
2 garlic cloves, peeled and minced
1 teaspoon dried oregano
1 tablespoon stone ground mustard
Salt and pepper to taste

## PROCEDURES

**1.** Bring a large pot with 3-4 quarts of water and one tablespoon of salt to a boil and add the Romanesco and broccoli florets. Return to a rolling boil. Cook for 5 minutes, drain, and rinse with cold water to stop the cooking and set the color.

**2.** Combine the Romanesco, broccoli, olives, and red bell peppers in a bowl and mix well.

**3.** Make the dressing by whisking together the olive oil, lemon juice, minced garlic, oregano, and mustard.

**4.** Pour the dressing over the salad, mix well, taste and add salt and pepper as desired.

# UN PO' PIÚ DIFICILE (A BIT MORE DIFFICULT)

These are the salads to try when you have a bit more time to cook. You might have to make some polenta and then fry it up, roast some vegetables, or grill some radicchio, but the results will impress.

# INSALATA CON AVOCADO E MANGO (AVOCADO AND MANGO SALAD)

Your knife skills may be tested a bit by this recipe because traditional methods don't cut it (ha) for mangos or avocados. For the avocado, I like to cut into the stem end with a sharp knife until I hit the seed, and then rotate the avocado so that the flesh and skin are cut in half but still attached to the seed. Then, in a vegan version of breaking a wishbone, twist the avocado and you will end up with two identical halves except that one holds the seed. Taking the seed-free half, gently make ten or so lengthwise cuts and scoop out the slices with a spoon (see the beginning of the *Un Po' Più Dificile* section of this book for a photo). Lay the other half (with the seed) on your cutting board, put your non-knife hand behind your back, and firmly strike the seed with your sharp knife (larger, heavier knives work better for this). With the knife embedded in the seed, hold and twist the avocado and the seed will come free. Carefully pull the seed off the knife and repeat slicing as before. For the mango, I find it easiest to cut a thin slice off the top and bottom and peel the skin with a vegetable peeler. Then you can take two large pieces off the sides of the flat seed. You can usually "see" the position of the flat seed as it is reflected in the shape of the fruit. Turn it until you are looking at the thinnest profile and you should be able to slice a large piece off the left and right sides. Thinly slice the side pieces for the salad (see the beginning of the *Facile* section of this book for a photo) and eat the delicious flesh around the seed. Don't worry if you mangle the mango, this salad is just as good no matter how you slice it!

## INGREDIENTS (2 MEALS OR 6 SIDES)

3 ounces baby arugula (or chopped arugula)
1 mature avocado, sliced
1 mature mango, sliced
½ red onion, peeled and sliced thinly
3 tablespoons olive oil
Juice of 1 lemon
¼ teaspoon crushed red pepper
Salt and pepper to taste
¼ cup walnuts, chopped and toasted

**1.** Combine the arugula, avocado, mango, and onion in a bowl and mix well.

**2.** Make the dressing by whisking together the olive oil, lemon juice, and crushed red pepper.

**3.** Drizzle the dressing over the salad, mix well, taste, and add salt and pepper as desired.

**4.** Garnish with the walnuts.

# INSALATA D'AUTUNNO
## (FALL SALAD)

The Italians have a saying: *avere sale in zucca*, meaning to have salt in your pumpkin. The pumpkin refers to the human brain, and the salt means that the person is quite clever. You could also say that someone has *poco* (little) *sale in zucca*, meaning they are not particularly bright. Well you would have plenty of salt in your pumpkin if you chose to make this salad in the fall when fresh pumpkins and squashes are available, which serendipitously coincides with the time when apples and cauliflower are also at their peak. This salad is a wonderful mixture of salty pumpkin, cauliflower (which also, coincidentally, looks like a brain), nuts, and fruits. Remember that dish you made with nuts and you were glad that you hadn't toasted them first? Me neither. So toast those hazelnuts in a 350-degree oven for about 10 minutes (shaking the pan a time or two) or in a frying pan on the stovetop at medium heat. Whenever I plan on toasting nuts for a recipe, I always buy twice the required amount in anticipation of burning the first batch. They go from raw to burnt *very* quickly (as I tell myself and anyone else in my kitchen who dares to complain about the smell of burnt nuts). Anyway, it's worth burning a few batches for the wonderful, aromatic, nutty flavor you can add to this salad or any dish.

## INGREDIENTS (2 MEALS OR 6 SIDES)

1 pound peeled, cleaned, and diced pumpkin (or butternut squash)
½ pound cauliflower, cleaned and diced
3 tablespoons olive oil (divided 1 + 2)
1½ cups cooked cannellini beans (or one 15-ounce can, drained and rinsed)
2 tart apples, cored and diced
2 tablespoons apple cider vinegar
Salt and pepper to taste
½ cup hazelnuts (preferably toasted), roughly chopped

## PROCEDURES

**1.** Mix the pumpkin, cauliflower, a pinch of salt, and one tablespoon of olive oil in an oven pan and bake at 350 degrees for about 30 minutes (stirring a few times for more even cooking) until the pumpkin and cauliflower are tender but not mushy (it's nice if the cauliflower has a bit of crunch left in it). Let the pumpkin and cauliflower cool to room temperature.

**2.** Combine the pumpkin, cauliflower, beans, and apple in a bowl and mix well.

**3.** Make the dressing by whisking together the remaining 2 tablespoons of olive oil and the vinegar.

**4.** Drizzle the dressing over the salad, mix well, taste, and add salt and pepper as desired.

**5.** Garnish with the chopped hazelnuts.

# INSALATA DI FAGIOLI MISTI E ZUCCA (MIXED BEAN AND PUMPKIN SALAD)

This is a beany-er and herby-er and less sweet version of the *Insalata d'Autunno*. The addition of the borlotti beans and herbs to the cannellini beans and pumpkin and the removal of the apples results in a more substantial and savory salad compared to the lighter and sweeter version. Depending on your tastes and moods, both versions are delicious and great dishes with which to use up those fall pumpkins and squashes. Both would also make great additions to a Thanksgiving or harvest festival table.

## INGREDIENTS (2 MEALS OR 6 SIDES)

1 pound peeled, cleaned, and diced pumpkin (or butternut squash)
½ yellow or white onion, peeled and diced
Leaves from 2 sprigs of rosemary, roughly chopped
1 tablespoon thyme leaves
3 tablespoons olive oil (divided 1 + 2)
1½ cups cooked cannellini beans (or one 15-ounce can, drained and rinsed)
1½ cups cooked borlotti (or pinto) beans (or one 15-ounce can, drained and rinsed)
3 ounces baby spinach
Juice of 1 lemon
Salt and pepper to taste

## PROCEDURES

**1.** Mix the pumpkin, onion, rosemary, thyme, and one tablespoon of olive oil in an oven pan and bake at 350 degrees for about 30 minutes (stirring a few times for even cooking) until the pumpkin is tender but not mushy.

**2.** Let the pumpkin cool to room temperature.

**3.** Combine the pumpkin, beans, and spinach in a bowl and mix well.

**4.** Make the dressing by whisking together the remaining 2 tablespoons of olive oil and the lemon juice.

**5.** Drizzle the dressing over the salad, mix well, taste, and add salt and pepper as desired.

# INSALATA DI RADICCHIO ALLA GRIGLIA
# (GRILLED RADICCHIO SALAD)

The radicchio in this bitter salad can be grilled or roasted and left large or chopped after cooking. It makes a beautiful presentation if unchopped but is easier to eat if the core is removed and the leaves are chopped after grilling, merely because it is easier for you to do with a chef's knife on a cutting board than for each person to do the same on a dinner plate (and presumably without a chef's knife). I use my panini press to grill the half-heads of radicchio, but they can certainly be done on an outdoor grill, on a grill pan, or in the oven (at 350 degrees, cut side oiled and down, for about 20 minutes). This salad can be served while the radicchio is still warm (my preference) or at room temperature.

## INGREDIENTS (2 MEALS OR 6 SIDES)

2 large radicchio heads, cut in half, rinsed and dried, but with the cores intact
3 tablespoons olive oil (divided 1 + 2)
½ cup green olives, pitted and sliced
½ cup black olives, pitted and sliced
¼ cup capers, drained
1 tablespoon dried oregano
¼ teaspoon crushed red pepper
Juice of ½ lemon
½ teaspoon of salt
½ teaspoon of pepper

## PROCEDURES

**1.** Drizzle or paint one tablespoon (total) of olive oil over the cut sides of the radicchio halves and grill for 5-10 minutes until well browned but still firm, and set aside.
**2.** Make the dressing by mixing the remaining 2 tablespoons of olive oil, olives, capers, oregano, crushed red pepper, lemon juice, salt, and pepper in a bowl.
**3.** Drizzle the dressing over the cooked radicchio (cut side up) and serve.
**4.** Sit back and bask in the glory.

# INSALATA DI PASTA
## (PASTA SALAD)

What better way could there be to pretend to be healthy (look Ma, I'm eating salad!) while consuming mass quantities of our favorite carbohydrate? The combination of the savory eggplant with the sweet and crunchy bell peppers is the perfect, well, let's face it, the perfect excuse to eat a bunch of pasta. The diet starts tomorrow.

## INGREDIENTS (2 MEALS OR 6 SIDES)

1 medium eggplant
4 tablespoons olive oil (divided 2 + 2)
6 ounces dry farfalle pasta (or other bite-sized pasta)
½ yellow bell pepper, diced small or julienned
½ red bell pepper, diced small or julienned
½ green bell pepper, diced small or julienned
2 garlic cloves, peeled and minced
½ teaspoon crushed red pepper
1 teaspoon dried oregano
2 tablespoon white wine vinegar
Salt and pepper to taste

## PROCEDURES

**1.** Cut the top and bottom off the eggplant and slice into ½" rounds. Brush each slice with olive oil (the first 2 tablespoons) and grill in batches for about 5-6 minutes per batch until cooked and nicely marked. I like to use my panini press, but a stovetop grill pan works well, or an outdoor grill. Alternatively, you can dice the eggplant, drizzle with olive oil, and bake for 30 minutes at 350 degrees, stirring a few times). Allow the eggplant to cool, and then roughly chop it if not already diced.
**2.** Boil the pasta in plenty of heavily salted water (1 tablespoon per quart of water) for 12 minutes; drain, rinse with cool water, and allow to dry for a minute or two.
**3.** Combine the eggplant, pasta, and bell peppers in a bowl and mix well.
**4.** Make the dressing by whisking together the remaining 2 tablespoons of olive oil, minced garlic, crushed red pepper, dried oregano, and vinegar.

**5.** Drizzle the dressing over the salad, mix well, taste, and add salt and pepper as desired.

# INSALATA ALLA POLENTONA
## (FRIED POLENTA SALAD)

Most of the salads in this book are light, healthy, packed with vitamins, minerals, antioxidants, and other helpful substances, and other salads are...this salad. You can use precooked tubes of polenta from the grocery store, and just skip the first three steps below. If you're trying to pack on the pounds before hibernation, the polenta can also be deep fried. Yikes!

## INGREDIENTS (2 MEALS OR 6 SIDES)

4 ounces coarse yellow cornmeal (polenta)
1 teaspoon salt
¼ cup vegetable oil (frying oil)
1½ cups cooked cannellini beans (or one 15-ounce can, drained and rinsed)
2 ounces baby greens (or field greens)
1 carrot, peeled and grated
1 celery stalk, diced
20 cherry or grape tomatoes, halved
¼ red onion, peeled and sliced thinly
2 tablespoons olive oil
2 tablespoons white wine vinegar
Salt and pepper to taste

## PROCEDURES

**1.** Bring 2 cups of water with 1 teaspoon of salt to a boil. Sprinkle in the cornmeal while whisking. Continue whisking for 5 minutes so the polenta does not clump. Regulate the heat so that when you stop whisking bubbles begin to appear after about 5 seconds. Swap out your whisk for a wooden spoon and continue cooking, stirring thoroughly and frequently for 20 more minutes or until the polenta is almost as thick as mashed potatoes.

**2.** Spread the polenta in an oiled, shallow pan at a thickness of about ½ inch, flattening the top with wetted fingers or a silicone spatula. Refrigerate uncovered until solidified (at least an hour).

**3.** Slice the chilled polenta into 1" squares. Pour the vegetable oil into a frying pan on medium heat until the oil shimmers and just begins to smoke. Giving each piece plenty of room, add the polenta in batches and don't touch them for 2 minutes (to avoid sticking). Fry until well browned on the bottom, flip carefully, and repeat. Remove each piece and place on a towel to cool. The pieces should stay crunchy for ½ hour or so.

**4.** Combine the beans, greens, carrot, celery, tomatoes, and onion in a bowl and mix well.

**5.** Make the dressing by whisking together the olive oil and vinegar.

**6.** Drizzle the dressing over the salad, mix well, taste, and add salt and pepper as desired.

**7.** Garnish each serving with plenty of polenta chunks.

**8.** Thank your lucky stars that someone once thought it might be a good idea to fry polenta.

Caesar
Salad

Fava Bean and Farro Salad

Scafata

# BONUS SALADS

I've included three bonus salads in this book because they are either not strictly Italian (Caesar Salad) or because they include an ingredient that is not readily accessible (why oh why aren't fresh fava beans available at every grocery store?!). Rest assured, these are not part of the 32-recipe set you paid good money for, but they are too good to leave out.

# INSALATA DI CAESAR (CAESAR SALAD)

I'd like to immediately debunk the rumor that this salad is nothing more than a crouton delivery system, but I can't. This salad is not Italian (despite what one would be led to believe in just about every Italian restaurant in America) and although it is vegan it is not accidentally so. But, it is fantastic, and so I have included it in the bonus section of this book. Tons of flavor. Tons of bite. Tons of...croutons. Most commercial "bacon" bits have nothing to do with bacon including the popular McCormick brand (it has always been soy-based, and don't let the lactic acid ingredient fool you, in this product it is derived from bacteria, not milk). If you're not sure, there are plenty of named vegan bacon substitutes available. The salad is also fantastic without this ingredient, but the smokey, salty vegan bacon is a nice addition. Speaking of salt, with the vegan bacon bits and vegan parmesan, you may not need any additional salt with this recipe (although a bit of pepper gives it a nice kick).

## INGREDIENTS (2 MEALS OR 6 SIDES)

4 slices of rustic bread (about 4 ounces), diced
4 tablespoons olive oil (divided 1 + 3)
2 heads of romaine lettuce, cored and chopped
½ cup vegan bacon bits
4 garlic cloves, peeled and minced
Juice of 2 lemons
2 tablespoons stone ground mustard
Salt and pepper to taste
½ cup vegan parmesan cheese of your choice

## PROCEDURES

**1.** Make the croutons by drizzling 1 tablespoon of olive oil over the diced bread, adding a pinch of salt and pepper, mixing, and baking in a 400-degree oven for about 10-12 minutes. Turn the croutons a couple of times to ensure even crunchiness. Allow to cool to room temperature.

**2.** Combine the lettuce, vegan bacon bits, and croutons in a bowl and mix well.

**3.** Make the dressing by whisking together the remaining 3 tablespoons of olive oil, minced garlic, lemon juice, and mustard.

**4.** Drizzle the dressing over the salad, mix well, taste, and add salt and pepper as desired.

**5.** Garnish with the vegan parmesan.

# INSALATA DI FAVA E FARRO
# (FAVA BEAN AND FARRO SALAD)

There are plenty of delicious dishes you can make with dried fava beans including soups and bread toppers (*companatici*), the subjects of current and future *Accidentally Vegan* books. However, this salad requires *fresh* fava beans which are, admittedly, somewhat difficult to find in certain areas. Your best bet is to grow your own or try to find them frozen at the grocery store. Italian, Middle Eastern, or North African specialty grocers are possibilities. Why go to all this trouble? The humble fava answers this question with a shockingly velvety texture and delectable flavor. When you are tired of chickpeas, kidney beans, and lentils, fresh fava beans can brighten up your vegan salad menu.

## INGREDIENTS (2 MEALS OR 6 SIDES)

1 cup uncooked farro
2 cups fresh fava beans
4 ounces bitter greens (such as chard, spinach, or kale), roughly chopped
2 tablespoons olive oil
1 tablespoon balsamic vinegar
Salt and pepper to taste
2 tablespoons chopped chives

## PROCEDURES

**1.** Bring two pots of water (about 1 quart each) to a boil and add a teaspoon of salt to each.

**2.** In one pot, add the fava beans. Cook for about 2 minutes, drain, and rinse with cold tap water.

**3.** In the other pot, stir in the farro, return to a simmer and cover, adjusting the heat so that it is barely simmering. Cook for 30 minutes (until the farro is tender but not mushy). Drain and rinse with cold tap water.

**4.** In the meantime, peel the skin from each fava bean, being careful not to crush the tender flesh inside.

**5.** Combine the farro, fava beans, and bitter greens in a bowl and mix well.

**6.** Make the dressing by whisking together the olive oil and vinegar.

**7.** Drizzle the dressing over the salad, mix well, taste, and add salt and pepper as desired.

**8.** Top with chopped chives.

# SCAFATA (FAVA BEAN AND ESCAROLE SALAD)

This recipe is in the bonus section of this book for two reasons. First, fresh fava beans can be difficult to find (the recipe for *Insalata di Fava e Farro* has some hints). Second, one could argue that this is not technically a salad as all of the ingredients (except the basil) are cooked. However, this Umbrian dish is full of greens and often eaten at room temperature or even cold. Since it doesn't fit in any other *Accidentally Vegan* book and is too good to ignore, I have included it here. Sue me now, thank me later. This salad can be eaten freshly prepared and still warm (my favorite), after it cools to room temperature (my favorite), or the next day from the refrigerator (my favorite).

## INGREDIENTS (2 MEALS OR 6 SIDES)

1 cup fresh fava beans
2 tablespoons olive oil
¼ red onion, peeled and sliced thinly
2 garlic cloves, peeled and minced
¼ teaspoon crushed red pepper
4 ounces escarole (or other bitter green), roughly chopped
1 cup fresh or frozen sweet peas
5 basil leaves, roughly chopped
Salt and pepper to taste

## PROCEDURES

**1.** Bring a pot of water (about 1 quart) to a boil and add a teaspoon of salt.

**2.** Add the fava beans and boil for about 2 minutes, drain, and rinse with cold tap water.

**3.** Peel the skin from each fava bean, being careful not to crush the tender flesh inside.

**4.** Add the olive oil, onion, and crushed red pepper to a large frying pan on medium low heat. Fry gently for about 5 minutes and then add the garlic, escarole, and sweet peas. Fry for an additional 3 minutes.

**5.** Add the peeled fava beans and basil to the pan, toss briefly, and remove from the heat.

**6.** Taste and add salt and pepper as desired.

Made in United States
Orlando, FL
07 August 2022